W9-APR-962

GOD is in the little things

A Sprig of Parsley

FaithKidz®
Equipping Kids for Life

An Imprint of Cook Communications Ministries
Colorado Springs, CO

Faith Parenting Guide
Ages 4-7
Appreciation

A Faith Parenting Guide
can be found starting on page 32

Written by Patricia Karwatowicz
Illustrated by Jane Dippold

Faith Kidz is an imprint of Cook Communications Ministries
Colorado Springs, Colorado 80918
Cook Communications, Paris, Ontario
Kingsway Communications, Eastbourne, England

A SPRIG OF PARSLEY © 2005 by Patricia Karwatowicz

All rights reserved. No part of this publication may be reproduced without written permission, except for brief quotations in books and critical reviews. For information, write Cook Communications Ministries, 4050 Lee Vance View, Colorado Springs, CO 80918.

All Scripture quotations, unless indicated, are taken from the NEW INTERNATIONAL VERSION®. NIV®. Copyright ©1995, 1996, 1998 by International Bible Society. Used by permission of Zondervan Publishing House. All rights reserved.

First printing, 2005
Printed in India.
1 2 3 4 5 6 7 8 9 10 Printing/Year 08 07 06 05

ISBN 078141153

Editor: Heather Gemmen
Design Manager: Nancy L. Haskins
Illustrator: Jane Dippold
Designer: Sandy Flewelling

To Frank,
my husband, soul-mate, and fellow gardener.
PK

Dedicated to my Grandma Pohl
JD

ROSES
5.95

4

The rose was $5.95. The daisy was $2.50.
Isabela didn't have enough money to buy Grammy's birthday present.

Mr. Sid, the owner of Sid's Garden Shop, saw Isabela's sad face,
so he handed her the last puny plant from the "Sale" table.

"It's only parsley," he said.
"Don't know if it'll grow."

"Thank you, Mr. Sid," Isabela said.
"God can make it grow."
And she skipped home
hugging her puny parsley plant.

Brendan Murphy skidded
to a stop on his skateboard.
"Boy!" he said, shaking his head.
"Your plant is droopy-loopy
and good for nothing."

9

"God made it," said Isabela,
"so there's lots of good in it."
But from then on
she propped up the puny parsley plant
with a popsicle stick
and tied it with a red ribbon.

The next day,
Isabela was swinging
in her porch swing,
admiring her plant,
when Amy zipped to a stop
on her bike.
"Plants can't grow
in the shade, Isabela,"
she said, shaking her head,
"It's too late now."

13

"It's never too late for God,"
said Isabela.
But from then on
she kept her plant in the sun.

The next day, Isabela sat on her swing,
admiring her plant,
when Mr. McGillicutty stopped by,
tapping his cane.
"Sorry, Isabela," he said,
shaking his head.
"You've given your plant too much water.
It's too late now."

"It's never too late for God,
Mr. McGillicutty."
But from then on
Isabela tested the soil with her finger
to see if it was too wet.

19

Even though her plant was a little sad,
it was the only present Isabela had
for Grammy's birthday.

Grammy smiled, shaking her head.
"Sometimes, Isabela,
we have to prune plants
to make them grow."
And she cut the parsley down
to a nubbin.

Every day, Isabela visited Grammy
and her puny parsley plant.
They watered it and propped it and kept it in the sun,
until one day it grew into a fine bushy plant
that smelled fresh and tingly.

Grammy cut snippets of fresh green parsley,
tied them with a red ribbon,
and let Isabela give them to her friends.

Mr. Sid
made parsley tea.

Brendan Murphy
munched parsley potatoes.

Mr. McGillicutty
sipped parsley soup.

Amy nibbled
parsley salad.

And Grammy made a parsley birthday cake—
only it wasn't really!
It was just a green cake
with a tiny parsley sprig on top.

"Never give up on God!"
said Isabela,
taking a big delicious bite.

"Every good and perfect gift is from above, coming down from the Father..."
James 1:17a

A Sprig of Parsley

AGES: 4-7

LIFE ISSUE: I want my children to enjoy what God has made.

SPIRITUAL BUILDING BLOCK: Appreciation

Do the following activities to help your children experience the goodness of God.

 SIGHT:

Go for a nature walk with your children. Have a treasure hunt for seeds—either on the ground on in plants. When you find a small seed, remind your children that Jesus said the tiniest mustard seed can grow into a large tree. Let your children choose a favorite plant as a reminder: Encourage them to remember God's love whenever they happen to see this plant.

A Sprig of Parsley

AGES: 4-7

LIFE ISSUE: I want my children to enjoy what God has made.

SPIRITUAL BUILDING BLOCK: Appreciation

Do the following activities to help your children experience the goodness of God.

 SOUND:

Take your children on a visit to a public garden, greenhouse, or nursery. Let them ask questions of an employee about how to care for plants. Then talk with your children about how we can help take care of God's plants by watering and fertilizing and weeding. Pull out a weed and examine the roots that receive water and food from the soil. Talk about how our spirits receive nourishment when we read the Bible and talk with God.

A Sprig of Parsley

AGES: 4-7

LIFE ISSUE: I want my child to enjoy what God has made.

SPIRITUAL BUILDING BLOCK: Appreciation

Do the following activities to help your child experience the goodness of God.

TOUCH:

Take your children to a place with a flower department in a grocery store. Ask them which flower has the softest petals, the prettiest design, or the most unusual shape. Let them look closely at a cactus and its prickles. Have them smell a few different plants. Talk about how God made each plant unique for a reason—some are beautiful to look at; some have built in protection; some have odors that repel leaf-eating bugs or attract pollinating bugs. Take a moment to thank God for making everything with a purpose.

God IS in the Little Things!
Get these titles by Patricia Karwatowicz.

A Child's Song
$12.99
10 x 8   Hardcover   36P
ISBN: 0-78144-116-1

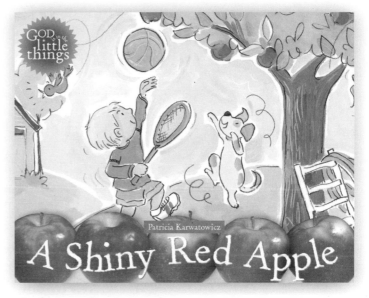

A Shiny Red Apple
$12.99
10 x 8   Hardcover   36P
ISBN: 0-78144-094-7

Get Your Copies Today! Order Online: www.cookministries.com, Phone: 1-800-323-7543
Or Visit your Local Christian Bookstore

The Word at Work Around the World

*W*hat would you do if you wanted to share God's love with children on the streets of your city? That's the dilemma David C. Cook faced in 1870's Chicago. His answer was to create literature that would capture children's hearts.

Out of those humble beginnings grew a worldwide ministry that has used literature to proclaim God's love and disciple generation after generation. Cook Communications Ministries is committed to personal discipleship—to helping people of all ages learn God's Word, embrace his salvation, walk in his ways, and minister in his name.

Faith Kidz, RiverOak, Honor, Life Journey, Victor, NextGen . . . every time you purchase a book produced by Cook Communications Ministries, you not only meet a vital personal need in your life or in the life of someone you love, but you're also a part of ministering to José in Colombia, Humberto in Chile, Gousa in India, or Lidiane in Brazil. You help make it possible for a pastor in China, a child in Peru, or a mother in West Africa to enjoy a life-changing book. And because you helped, children and adults around the world are learning God's Word and walking in his ways.

Thank you for your partnership in helping to disciple the world. May God bless you with the power of his Word in your life.

For more information about our international ministries,
visit www.ccmi.org.